The Lake District

Edward Alan Bowness

'The loveliest spot that man hath ever found.'

William Wordsworth

The Lake District became a National Park in 1951, and with an area of almost 900 square miles (2330 sq. km), it is the largest in England and Wales. Originally composed of three counties, Cumberland, Westmorland and the Furness district of Lancashire, all that is best in Lakeland is now within the new county of Cumbria. More picturesque and diverse scenery can be found here than in any comparable area of Britain. Its beauty is, above all, a beauty of contrasts.

Within 30 miles (48 km) one may range from the harsh crags of England's highest mountain, Scafell Pike, to the fertile lowland valleys around Winster, from the depths of great lakes like Windermere to shallow blue tarnlets scattered like confetti on the top of Haystacks, from sparkling ghylls on the side of Harrison Stickle to the roaring brown torrent of Duddon in flood.

But what, apart from scenery, does Lakeland offer to the holidaymaker? Some come for the quiet delights of trout-fishing at the head of Windermere late on a June evening, as the sun sets between the twin peaks of the Langdales and the water becomes a black mirror. Others revel in the kaleidoscope of colour and noise which is a Lakeland sports meeting at Grasmere or Ambleside. In Langdale, expert cragsmen test their muscles, skill and courage against the rock faces of Gimmer or Pavey Ark, or cut January steps into frozen snow cornices on Bowfell.

FRONT COVER: *Friar's Crag and Derwentwater, with Causey Pike in the distance.* ABOVE: *Derwentwater and Skiddaw in winter.* BACK COVER: *A winter sunset across the head of Lake Windermere. (All photographs are by the author unless otherwise acknowledged.)*

The cry of foxhounds, baying hotfoot across the slopes of Mellbreak, is music for many, whilst another makes a quiet annual pilgrimage each daffodil time to Dora's Field at Rydal.

Tradition dies hard in the Lakeland valleys, where fell racing and wrestling may still be found, and where the ancient rush-bearing ceremony continues each summer at Grasmere and Ambleside.

For the lover of outdoor life, the Lake District has almost everything. The camper, the artist, the pony-trekker, the yachtsman, the fisherman, the naturalist – Lakeland caters for them all. Go in June through Manesty Woods on Derwentwater's shore, and you would swear that nowhere could show so many shades of green. Visit again in October, and see the fox-red bracken above Watendlath, flaming in autumn sunshine. There are few finer days than those spent wandering the fells, to descend at dusk to a welcoming farmhouse and enjoy Cumbrian food and hospitality.

Much has been omitted, for each visitor has his own favourite mountain or valley, lake or tarn, and it is impossible to include them all. Some of the photographs may introduce readers to new aspects of the Lakeland scene, or serve as reminders of former delights. Make your own memories, on foot if you can, when the June days are long, the clouds are high and the hills are free. Perhaps then you may say of Lakeland, as William Wordsworth wrote of Grasmere, that it is 'the loveliest spot that man hath ever found'.

ABOVE: *Dow Crag and Coniston Old Man, viewed from the east shore of Coniston Water.* RIGHT: *Lakeland activities: Ponytrekking at Red Bank, Grasmere; Trout fishing on the River Brathay near Skelwith; A yacht jetty at the south end of Ullswater, near Patterdale village; A halt near Beckfoot on the narrow-gauge railway route up the Eskdale valley; Artists in Great Langdale; Fell walkers above Grasmere, looking towards Fairfield and Helvellyn, on a path over Huntingstile towards Elterwater.*

Kendal

Less than a mile (1·6 km) outside the National Park, Kendal is the main gateway to the Lakes for most travellers who come from the south. Now a prosperous town of more than 20,000 people, its turbulent history is suggested by the many narrow courtyards which lead off the main street. These are reputed to have been constructed so that defence was easy in the time of border raids from Scotland. The ruined castle where Catherine Parr, sixth wife of Henry VIII, was born is a notable viewpoint, standing dominant on a green hill above the town. The grey limestone buildings of old Kendal cling together on the steep fellside to the west of the town. The River Kent, claimed to be one of the swiftest rivers in England, divides the town with its north-to-south course from the hills above Kentmere to its estuary in Morecambe Bay.

There are many spots in Kendal worthy of mention. The fine parish church of the Holy Trinity, which dates back to the 13th century, is to the south of the town, and with its five aisles is one of the widest in the country. A musical carillon of tuneful bells can be heard marking the passing hours at the Town Hall. Pleasant riverside walks may be enjoyed at Gooseholme and in Abbot Hall Park. Here there is also a good art gallery and the Museum of Lakeland Life and Industry. The latter illustrates changes in rural and urban life in Lakeland over the past 200 years. Traditional rural trades such as those of the blacksmith and wheelwright are shown, while frequently changing exhibitions feature modern local industries. Two rooms are furnished in the style of the early 1900s, with costumes and household equipment of that period. In all, one can conjure up a fascinating picture of the region as it used to be. The standard of excellence may be judged from the fact that the museum was a former winner of the Museum of the Year award.

The thriving industries of the town today range from shoe-making to engineering, from snuff-manufacture to mint-cake production, and include pottery, printing, carpet-weaving and knitting. The two latter trades are a reminder of the medieval prosperity of Kendal as a major centre of woollen cloth production.

Two weeks in August and September are perhaps the highlight of the year in modern Kendal. The Kendal Gathering is held then, a succession of entertainments ranging from visits by TV personalities to competitions to find local superstars, from celebrity piano recitals to youth band concerts. The climax comes with the famous torchlight procession, when thousands of marchers and decorated floats parade round the town. The event is claimed to be one of the most spectacular in England, taking over an hour to pass any one place on the route.

Each summer in Kendal sees the Cumbria Steam Gathering, which usually attracts exhibits from all over the country. The grand parade of mobile steam-engines is a brilliant presentation of fairground engines, steam-rollers and steam-driven farm machinery. The event takes place at the Westmorland County Showfield, on the northern edge of Kendal.

4

Brockhole

The Lake District National Park Centre is located at Brockhole, on the A591 road roughly halfway between Ambleside and Windermere. Opened in 1969 as the first of its kind in England, the aim of the Centre is to increase visitor appreciation of the National Park. A unique exhibition illustrates the natural and human changes which have contributed to the evolution of the Lake District into what it is today. From March to November a series of talks and films are regularly given, interspersed from time to time with special topics and celebrity lectures. There are extensive grounds of over 30 acres (12 ha) which sweep down to the lake shore. Formal gardens, open grassy picnic areas and a self-guided lakeshore walk are all included. Trips may be taken by boat to Brockhole from Bowness and Waterhead, and the views across Windermere to the central Lakeland fells are magnificent. A visit to Brockhole is an attractive outing in glorious surroundings which should contribute greatly towards the enjoyment of a holiday.

ABOVE LEFT: *A quiet corner of old Kendal, off Abbot Hall Park, near the parish church.* LEFT: *Cherry blossom beside the River Kent at Kendal.* ABOVE: *Brockhole, the Visitor Centre for the Lake District National Park.* RIGHT: *Lake Windermere and Langdale Pikes, seen from the terrace at Brockhole.*

5

Windermere, Bowness and Ambleside

For many visitors the first sight of a lake is Winder-mere, a wide blue ribbon spread out below Claife Heights, viewed from the A591 road from Kendal. More than 10 miles (16 km) long, a mile (1·6 km) across, and over 200 feet (60 m) deep, it is by far the greatest natural expanse of fresh water in England. Users of the lake vary from motor vessels – *Swan*, *Teal* and *Tern* – to small rowing-boats and self-drive motor-boats which may be hired at Waterhead, Bowness and Lake Side. A busy cross-lake car ferry operates a regular service at the narrowest point of the lake near Bowness, giving most attractive access to roads on the western shore leading to Sawrey and Hawkshead.

The fisherman may pursue his trout, perch, pike and char in Windermere, and countless yachts, speed-boats and water-skiers make the lake alive with an ever-changing panorama of colour. Cross-lake and long-distance swims are held annually, whilst fishery research is carried on at the headquarters of the Freshwater Biological Association, Ferry House. The purity and volume of the water has made the lake attractive as a reservoir, and a discreetly hidden pumping station allows Manchester to draw water when required.

Several of the low hills around Windermere provide excellent viewpoints, notably Orrest Head, with a panoramic view of south Lakeland, and Gummer's How near the foot of Windermere lake. Both offer one of the easiest walks to an impressive viewpoint that can be found anywhere in the Lake District. Nearer to Windermere town itself, the National Trust property of Queen Adelaide's Hill (named in honour of a visit by William IV's widow) overlooks the middle of the lake.

The two neighbouring towns of Windermere and Bowness make up one of the most popular resorts within the National Park. Here there are craft shops in abundance, tea-rooms, high-class hotels and accom-modation of all types. Putting, tennis and miniature golf can be enjoyed, with parks and gardens close to the lake shore. At Bowness the ancient St Martin's church has notable stained glass, including the coat of arms of John Washington, later to be used in the American 'Stars and Stripes' flag.

Ambleside and Waterhead, at the north end of the lake, lie close to the site of the Roman fort, Galava. Again, holidaymakers will find plentiful and varied accommodation here, catering for those who wish to visit such features as Bridge House and Stock Ghyll waterfalls. A rush-bearing ceremony is held each summer, and later in the season the popular Ambleside sports meeting is held in Rydal Park.

ABOVE LEFT: *Dinghy sailors at Bowness Bay prepare their boats for sailing. A regular racing programme is held on Windermere throughout the season.* FAR LEFT: *The boat landings at Water-head on Lake Windermere, in autumn.* LEFT: *The gardens of the Lakeland Horticultural Society, Holehird, near Windermere.* ABOVE RIGHT: *Tulip time at the Promenade Gardens, Bowness on Windermere.* RIGHT: *Bridge House, Ambleside, a unique 16th-century building on a bridge over Stock Ghyll.*

7

Lakeland Sports

At one time, each village held its annual sports. Although this is not always the case now, there are few Saturdays in July and August when sports meetings cannot be found somewhere in Cumbria. The traditional events are fell racing, wrestling and hound-trailing.

The Fell or Guides Race is a race up the steepest nearby mountain from a flat arena in the valley bottom. A stern test of stamina and courage, the climb to the top of Butter Crags at Grasmere takes ten minutes, and the descent two and a half. Almost a vertical obstacle race, walls, gates, bracken and rocks have all to be negotiated at top speed.

Wrestling in Cumberland and Westmorland style is carried out in traditional costume. This consists of long white tights, velvet pants and a sleeveless vest. Ornate embroidery covers the costume, and competitions for the best and neatest outfit are often held prior to the actual wrestling. World Championships are fought for on the green turf of the valleys, where an 18-stone (114 kg) farmer will begin his bout with the balance and precision of a ballet dancer. The hold for the contest is with the head on the right shoulder of your opponent, and hands clasped tightly behind his back. A split second of violent action, and one man flies

through the air. The contest ends when one of the contestants is on the ground, victim perhaps of a hank, a back heel, or an inside hype.

Hound-trailing has been a popular pastime for many years, and the sport is governed by the Hound Trailing Association, which authorises fixtures throughout the summer. The trail is laid by two men, starting at the centre and working outwards to start and finish, and dogs are trained to follow the scent. The course may be as long as 10 miles (16 km), crossing becks, ghylls and rocks over some of the highest mountains in England. At the start and finish the baying of the hounds merges with the whistles and shouts of the owners to form part of an unforgettable scene.

ABOVE LEFT: *Fred Reeves of Coniston leads over the first wall on the climb of Butter Crags in the Grasmere Fell Race.* BOTTOM LEFT: *Tommy Sedgwick of New Hutton, famous athlete of the Grasmere Fell Race, shows the style of a champion in the Wasdale Head Fell Race, against the background of the Scafell range.* CENTRE: *The trailer returns after dragging his cloth, soaked in aniseed and paraffin, for five miles over the hills to lay a trail for the hounds to follow.* ABOVE: *The hounds are slipped at the start of the trail.* RIGHT: *Wrestling in Cumberland and Westmorland style at the Lowick Show, near Coniston Water, showing a well-known expert, Tom Harrington of Carlisle.*

Grasmere and Rydal

Wordsworth and Grasmere are inseparable. From 1799 to 1808 Dove Cottage was the home of the premier poet of Lakeland. Here William Wordsworth wrote some of his greatest poetry, and enjoyed by simple country living perhaps the happiest years of his life. Now owned by the Trustees of Dove Cottage, this Lakeland house of stone, plaster and whitewashed walls has been preserved largely as it was in the days when Wordsworth lived there. Much original furniture has been retained, and the Wordsworth Museum a few yards away houses priceless manuscripts and some first editions of the poet's work. Many household objects of the district are included, with part of the display featuring a typical Westmorland farm kitchen of the period.

The placid lake and surrounding hills were a source of inspiration to the poet, and walks in the Grasmere area are particularly rewarding. A circuit of the lake may be made, whilst the easy stroll to White Moss Common opens up viewpoints from which both Grasmere lake and Rydal Water may be seen. The valley walk towards lonely Easedale Tarn is a popular route, especially when the tumbling waterfalls of Sourmilk Ghyll are in spate.

The well-known silhouette of Helm Crag has been aptly named 'The Lion and the Lamb', from the strangely shaped boulders at the top. Other peaks near Grasmere are Fairfield, 2863 feet (872 m), and Helvellyn, 3113 feet (948 m), with mountain passes for hikers leading to Patterdale and Ullswater.

On the Saturday nearest to St Oswald's Day (5 August) visitors to Grasmere are numbered in thousands. Their goal is the centuries-old rush-bearing ceremony. This probably dates from the period when rushes were brought from fields and lakeside to cover the church floor before winter. Today it is a purely decorative procession around the village, with brilliant garlands of flowers added to the green rushes. The church banner of St Oswald heads the ceremonial walk, with children in green costumes and white-robed clergymen adding further touches of brilliance to this colourful scene.

Two miles (3 km) from Grasmere, the tiny village of Rydal is again associated with Wordsworth. Rydal Mount was his home from 1813 to 1850, and a field of daffodils, named in memory of Wordsworth's daughter Dora, can be found beside the road from Ambleside to Grasmere. The house itself contains family portraits, first editions and personal possessions of the poet, in a fine setting of landscaped gardens overlooking the Vale of Rydal.

ABOVE LEFT: *Grasmere lake and village, viewed from Red Bank.* FAR LEFT: *Dove Cottage, Grasmere, home of the poet William Wordsworth from 1799 to 1808.* LEFT: *The entrance porch at Rydal Mount, where Wordsworth lived from 1813 until his death in 1850.* ABOVE: *Village children assemble with their garlands before the Grasmere rush-bearing ceremony.*

11

Coniston, Hawkshead and Tarn Hows

Copper-mining and slate-quarrying have long been associated with Coniston; today only the latter continues, but lovers of industrial archaeology will find much to interest them amongst the disused – and dangerous – mine workings on the slopes of Coniston Old Man. The lake at Coniston is world-famous as the venue for water speed-boat record attempts, first by Sir Malcolm Campbell before the Second World War and later by his son Donald. A green stone memorial in Coniston village perpetuates the memory of the latter, killed in a high-speed crash whilst attempting a new record.

When life' moved at a more leisurely pace, Brantwood, on the eastern shore of Coniston Water, was the home of the celebrated Victorian poet, artist and writer, John Ruskin, who lived here for 28 years. The house is now preserved with much of his furniture, pictures and books, and is open for visitors throughout the year. A nature trail has been made in the extensive estate, and with its great variety of woodland, stream and fell, is said to be one of the finest in the Lake District.

The attractive village of Hawkshead lies in the next valley. Here you will find a unique fairyland of houses and cottages, packed tightly together with narrow streets and courtyards between. External steps and stairs lead to upper storeys, with quaint archways over the lanes around the square. William Wordsworth went to the grammar school here, and lodged in Ann Tyson's cottage not far away. A former prosperous centre of the medieval woollen industry, Hawkshead is dominated by its church, standing on a low hill above the village.

Near Sawrey provides another literary association, for here, at Hill Top Farm, lived Beatrix Potter. She was a lifelong supporter of the National Trust, to whom she left much Lakeland property.

Near Hawkshead one finds the beautiful National Trust property of Tarn Hows. This upland tarn looks so much part of its wooded surroundings that it is hard to believe that it was created by damming a small stream. Edged with conifers and with circling footpaths, it provides some of the finest panoramic views towards the main Lakeland fells. From here, Coniston Old Man, Wetherlam, the Langdale Pikes and Helvellyn are some of the peaks which may be seen across the blue waters of the tarn.

From Hawkshead a fascinating visit can be made to the Forestry Commission Visitor and Wildlife Centre at Grizedale, on the Hawkshead to Satterthwaite road. Facilities available in this 8000-acre (3236 ha) forest include exhibitions of forestry and woodland life, observation hides, forest walks, a camp site, self-catering accommodation and a small theatre.

ABOVE LEFT: *Tarn Hows and the Helvellyn range.* FAR LEFT: *The peace of an autumn afternoon at Waterhead, Coniston Water.* LEFT: *One of many attractive picnic spots along the east shore of Coniston Water.* TOP RIGHT: *Sailing at the south end of Coniston Water.* CENTRE RIGHT: *The old grammar school, Hawkshead, where William Wordsworth was a pupil.* RIGHT: *St Michael's church, Hawkshead.*

13

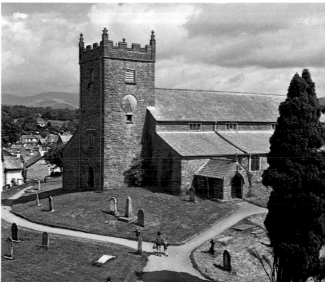

MOUNTAIN SAFETY

WEAR: Brightly coloured, wind-and-rain-proof cloth-ing. Boots with nails or moulded-rubber Vibram-type soles are essential.

TAKE: Map, compass, whistle, torch, spare food, warm clothing, watch, first-aid and at least one com-panion.

KNOW: How to use your map and compass, what time it gets dark and the distress signal for use in an emergency (six long blasts or flashes repeated at one-minute intervals).

TELL: Someone where you are going, and when and where you intend to return.

AVOID: Precipices, icy slopes, loose boulders, gullies and stream beds, over-confidence and carelessness.

Fell-walking and Rock-climbing

British mountaineering owes much to Lakeland, where the sport was pioneered on the fells and crags more than 100 years ago. The most popular valleys for climbers are Langdale, Wasdale, Borrowdale and Eskdale, lying at the foot of the major mountains and with easy routes to the principal rock faces.

Fell-walking, with care, lies within the ability of most from seven to seventy who are reasonably fit, but rock-climbing calls for a special breed of men and women. Strength, balance, iron nerves and immaculate judgement are all needed if Dow Crag, Pavey Ark and Napes Needle are to be conquered. An apprenticeship should be served on easy beginners' climbs before the extremely severe ones are attempted, for such climbs stretch the best of each generation to the limit of their ability.

Most of the classic rock climbs lie west of a line from Ambleside to Keswick, using largely the crags of Borrowdale volcanic rock. This surface is often rough, giving good hand- and foot-grip on massive precipices of sound rock, where the climber can, usually, be sure that his hold is not going to crumble. Semi-alpine conditions occur in winter, when work on snow and ice in north-facing gullies is a task for the expert.

Inevitably the challenge of the hills has brought competition, and for fell-walkers the supreme test is the Bob Graham Round. This involves climbing more than 40 Lakeland peaks over a distance of 75 miles (120 km), and with 27,000 feet (8229 m) of ascent and descent. The record time for the circuit stands at 13 hours 54 minutes!

Going on the fells can never be without hazard, and one of the pioneers of climbing gave his opinion thus: 'Courage and strength are nought without prudence; do nothing in haste; look well to each step; and from the beginning, think what may be the end.' Mountain rescue on the hills is now highly organised, with voluntary search and rescue teams based at many points accessible to the hills. The fact that the Langdale/Ambleside group of almost 50 climbers was called out to the great number of 54 rescues in 1984 indicates the importance of this work. Highly mobile, with land-rovers and extensive rescue equipment available, the teams co-operate with RAF helicopter services, so that rapid recovery is possible and transport is on hand for the removal of injured climbers to hospital.

Provided the visitor treats them with respect, however, the mountains can afford hours of immense enjoyment.

FAR LEFT: *Climbing on Raven Crag, Great Langdale (photograph by John Fell).* ABOVE LEFT: *Winter conditions above Harrop Tarn, looking towards the snow-covered Helvellyn range.* CENTRE: *A mountain-rescue vehicle on exhibition at the Ambleside sports meeting.* ABOVE: *Great Gable, viewed across Innominate Tarn on the summit of Haystacks.*

Langdale, Loughrigg and Elterwater

The Langdale valley is generally recognised as one of the finest in Lakeland, and with easy access from the south through Ambleside it is one of the most popular holiday areas. Beyond Skelwith Bridge, with its well-known waterfall, the road winds through leafy woodlands above the shores of Elterwater Tarn.

A diversion from Skelwith Bridge along the lower slopes of Loughrigg Fell leads to Loughrigg Tarn, a tiny mirror-like sheet of water almost encircled by trees, and with a popular footpath along the shore. Walkers may continue via Loughrigg Terrace to Grasmere or Rydal, whilst the motorist may descend Red Bank into Grasmere, or return to the Langdale valley at Elterwater. The village green here encircles a picturesque maple tree.

From all directions, the twin peaks of the Langdale Pikes dominate the scene. Not high, even by Lakeland standards, at 2403 feet (732 m), the slopes rise abruptly from the level valley floor at Dungeon Ghyll, and their craggy outlines form a characteristic view even when seen from 10 miles (16 km) or more distant.

The village houses at Elterwater and Chapel Stile are built from grey-green stone quarried in the valley, where the slate industry has been the main occupation for centuries. Stone in Langdale was worked 5000 years ago at a Stone Age axe factory situated near Pike of Stickle, and axes have been found at various sites throughout England. Now in the 20th century the

Langdale stone goes even further afield, for Spout Crag and Elterwater slate and stone are found on buildings the world over.

It is hard to imagine that the peaceful village of Elterwater was once a noted centre for gunpowder-making, using water-power from the river and local charcoal from the surrounding coppice woods.

From Chapel Stile the road winds westwards to Dungeon Ghyll. This is another famous rock-climbing centre, with Gimmer Crag and Pavey Ark near at hand. For the fell-walker there is the circuit of the Langdale horseshoe around Bowfell and Harrison Stickle.

A steep mountain pass over Blea Tarn links the valleys of Great and Little Langdale, with a narrow switchback-like road, and passing places here and there. The blue waters of Blea Tarn gleam invitingly against the dark crags of Blake Rigg, and Blea Tarn house is passed by the roadside, the home of 'The Solitary' in Wordsworth's poem *The Excursion*.

ABOVE LEFT: *A winter scene at Elterwater Tarn, with the snow-capped Langdale Pikes in the distance.* LEFT: *Lingmoor Fell, Bowfell and Harrison Stickle.* TOP RIGHT: *Blea Tarn and the Langdale Pikes.* CENTRE RIGHT: *The village green at Elterwater.* RIGHT: *Wrynose Pass and Wet Side Edge viewed across Elterwater Tarn from the lower slopes of Loughrigg.*

Steam in Lakeland

Perhaps in reaction against the pace of modern living, there seems to be increasing nostalgia for the more leisurely steam travel of former years. In Lakeland both railway and boat enthusiasts are well catered for.

A visit to the Ravenglass and Eskdale miniature railway is a fascinating glimpse of the age of steam. This 15-inch (381 mm) gauge line, almost 7 miles (11 km) in length, is the successor to trains of 3-foot (914 mm) gauge which ran over 100 years ago. Today the route from Ravenglass to Dalegarth is served by four steam engines, picturesquely named after three rivers which meet at Ravenglass. The *River Esk*, *River Irt* and *River Mite*, joined recently by the *Northern Rock*, provide a unique trip on a narrow-gauge steam line from the sea to the foothills of great mountains.

For the boat enthusiast, the place to go is Windermere Steamboat Museum. Opened by Prince Charles in 1977, this is a collection of early steam craft. Pride of place probably goes to the steam-launch *Dolly*, built around 1850, and generally recognised as the oldest mechanically propelled boat in the world. Second to her is the steam-yacht *Esperance*, the oldest boat on Lloyd's Yacht Register; for elegance, the 80-year-old steam-launch *Branksome* must lead, with woodwork in teak and walnut, and with its original velvet and leather upholstery. Up to 30 boats can be berthed in the steamboat dock, and a large display area around provides additional information.

For standard-gauge steam trains one must visit the south end of Lake Windermere at Lake Side. Here is the terminus of the $3\frac{1}{2}$-mile (5 km) long Haverthwaite

to Newby Bridge railway. From this branch line of the former Furness Railway, trains connect at Lake Side with Sealink vessels on Lake Windermere, giving an attractive route into Lakeland.

No steam enthusiast visiting Lakeland should omit a visit to Steamtown at Carnforth. This is the largest mainline steam locomotive depot in Britain. Normally more than 20 British and Continental mainline and industrial locomotives are on view, with some 'in steam' at weekends from March to October. The mile (1·6 km) long site includes some of the working equipment of the former Carnforth Motive Power Depot, one of the last railway areas in the country to retain steam locomotives. The Cumbria Steam Gathering at Kendal (*see page* 4) commonly attracts over 500 exhibits.

FAR LEFT: *Some of the Windermere Steamboat Museum's vessels tied up at their piers on Lake Windermere.* TOP CENTRE: *The interior of the boathouse at the Windermere Steamboat Museum.* TOP RIGHT: *A standard-gauge steam train leaves Haverthwaite on its journey to Lake Side.* CENTRE: *A fine point for discussion between experts at the Kendal Steam Gathering.* ABOVE: *'Northern Rock' waits at Dalegarth on the Ravenglass and Eskdale railway, making steam for its journey from the mountains to the sea.*

Eskdale and the Duddon Valley

Two of the finest beauty spots of western Lakeland are provided by the Duddon and Eskdale valleys. Unusually for Lakeland, they are both lakeless, but make up for this by their streams, which are like mountain torrents. Both rise in the highest fells in the heart of the Lake District, cascading down to the sea in a series of gorges, waterfalls and plunge pools. Crystal-clear, with every stone visible on the stream bed, they provide along their banks some of the most attractive picnic spots that one could find when yellow gorse spills over the river-worn boulders in June, or brown bracken enriches the valleys on a fine October day.

Between the two valleys one can travel the renowned Hardknott Pass, with hairpin bends and one-in-three gradients, a test for both car and driver. Alongside the road on the Eskdale side is the ruined fort of Mediobogdum, home of a Roman garrison almost 2000 years ago. At the corners where its stone walls meet are the remains of watchtowers and near the main entrance the ruins of a bathhouse can be seen.

At the mouth of the Esk is the attractive little harbour of Ravenglass, with colour-washed cottages huddled together near the shore. The Ravenglass dunes were established as a nature reserve in 1954, and now support the largest colony of black-headed gulls in England. Other breeding birds include Sandwich and Arctic terns, shelducks and oystercatchers.

TOP: *Birks Bridge on the River Duddon.* ABOVE: *The Roman fort of Hardknott Castle, or Mediobogdum. The background hills are England's highest, the Scafell range.*

Wasdale

This remote western valley has many claims to fame. England's highest mountain peak, Scafell Pike, at 3206 feet (977 m), is adjacent to the shores of the deepest lake, Wastwater, 258 feet (78 m) deep. On the southeast side the famous screes sweep down from Illgill Head into the depths of the lake, while the opposite western shore is a place for outings and picnics as the July sun warms rocks and shingle.

Always one's view is drawn towards the circling peaks at the valley head, Yewbarrow, Kirk Fell, Great Gable and Scafell, the epitome of Lakeland landscape. It came as no surprise to lovers of the hills when this view of Wastwater and Gable was chosen as the emblem of the Lake District National Park.

The hamlet of Wasdale Head is a Mecca for fell-walkers and mountaineers. High-level passes lead to the Ennerdale, Buttermere, Borrowdale, Langdale and Eskdale valleys, whilst top-grade rock climbs on Pillar, Gable and Scafell are all within easy reach. A fine horseshoe circuit for experienced walkers is the route round Mosedale, starting near the narrow packhorse bridge behind the hotel. One of Lakeland's smallest churches is found at Wasdale Head, flanked by its sheltering yew trees in a setting of supreme mountain grandeur. Many of the memorials in its tiny churchyard bear witness to the fatal fascination which the surrounding peaks have exercised over climbers.

TOP: *Yewbarrow, Great Gable and the Scafell range, some of England's highest mountains viewed across its deepest lake, Wastwater.* ABOVE: *A packhorse bridge at Wasdale Head, leading westwards into Mosedale.*

Buttermere and Crummock Water

Twin lakes sharing the same valley, Buttermere and Crummock Water will appeal especially to the lover of peace and quiet. No power-boats disturb their surface, although rowing-boats, canoes and small sailing craft are permitted. The approach from Borrowdale via Honister Pass, which is 1176 feet (358 m) above sea-level, passes one of Lakeland's highest youth hostels, whilst on the left the face of Honister Crag has been honeycombed with caves and tunnels through years of slate-quarrying here.

The Honister summit is now widely used as a starting-point for many fell walks; the route to Great Gable from here is popular, and there is an easy climb with many rewarding views to the tarn-studded summit of nearby Haystacks.

Fleetwith Pike towers above the pass as it nears Buttermere, one of the circle of fells around the twin lakes. High Crag, High Stile and Red Pike lie to the west, whilst Robinson, Whiteless Pike and Grasmoor match them in grandeur on the east. Nearby Scale Force is a well-known destination for excursions from Buttermere village, and its waterfall of 120 feet (36 m) is one of the highest in Lakeland. North of Crummock the gentler landscape of the Vale of Lorton is soon visible, and the blue gem of little Loweswater lies beside a minor road leading westwards.

ABOVE: *Autumn sunlight on beeches at Buttermere.* TOP CENTRE: *Buttermere and Crummock Water viewed from the track to Haystacks.* TOP RIGHT: *Looking north along the shore of Crummock Water.* RIGHT: *High Crag from the summit of Haystacks.*

Keswick, Derwentwater and Watendlath

Keswick is by far the most popular centre from which to visit the northern part of Lakeland. Its beauty, like that of many of the larger towns of the region, lies more in its surroundings than in the town itself. Few spots in England can be more attractively placed, for it lies at the foot of Skiddaw and extends almost to the shore of Derwentwater. A prominent feature in the town centre is the Moot Hall, constructed over 100 years ago on the site of an earlier 16th-century foundation. It may once have been the local gaol and has certainly been a market hall, but today it is a tourist information centre.

Good accommodation is plentiful in Keswick, ranging from high-class hotels to modest bed-and-breakfast establishments. In July the town is especially crowded, when the Keswick Convention attracts clergymen and church people from all over the world.

Many literary figures are associated with Keswick, as manuscripts in the town's Fitz Park Museum remind us. The 18th and 19th centuries saw the first notable authors 'discovering' Lakeland, with Coleridge living at Keswick in 1800, followed three years later by the poet Robert Southey. Other famous visitors at this period include Shelley, Scott, Hazlitt and Lamb, seeking perhaps the peace so well portrayed by Thomas Gray, writing in 1769: 'In the evening walked alone down to the lake after sunset and saw the solemn colouring of night draw on, the last gleam of sunshine fading away on the hilltops, the deep serene of the waters, and the long shadows of the mountains.'

The shore of Derwentwater is little over a quarter of a mile (0·4 km) from the town. Here the National Trust owns the famous beauty spot of Friar's Crag, which provides fine views across the lake to the Borrowdale valley and to the highest mountains of central Lakeland. Memorials to John Ruskin, the writer, and Canon Rawnsley, one of the National Trust's founders, are located on the craggy headland amongst the pine trees.

Swimming, fishing and boating may all be enjoyed at Derwentwater, or walking to easily accessible beauty spots nearby such as Castle Head, from the summit of which there is a fine view of the lake, or the Lodore Falls. Incidentally, the climb to Skiddaw – 3053 feet (930 m) – is certainly the easiest way of reaching a summit above 3000 feet (914 m) in Lakeland.

From Keswick a popular excursion is to the hamlet of Watendlath, used by the late Sir Hugh Walpole as the background setting for his ever-popular *Herries Chronicles* series of novels. Leaving Keswick for Borrowdale, the B5289 road forks after 2 miles (3·2 km), with the minor left-hand road heading for Watendlath. On the way the famous Ashness Bridge is reached, beloved of artists and photographers. Shortly afterwards, a detour on the right leads to a wooded precipice, popularly known as 'Surprise View'. The crag falls almost to the shore of Derwentwater, with cars and motor-launches appearing as toys, hundreds of feet below. The tiny hamlet of Watendlath itself lies, encircled by fells, in a hidden valley beside the tarn of the same name. From Watendlath there is a popular footpath over the hills to Rosthwaite in Borrowdale.

TOP LEFT: *Ashness Bridge and Skiddaw.* ABOVE: *'Surprise View', looking across Derwentwater to Skiddaw from near the Watendlath road.* ABOVE RIGHT: *A packhorse bridge at St John's in the Vale, near Keswick.* RIGHT: *The hamlet and tarn at Watendlath.* FAR RIGHT: *Castlerigg stone circle, near Keswick, looking towards Blencathra. The 38 great boulders form the Lake District's most important prehistoric monument.*

Farming in Lakeland

Today's landscape in the valley heads of Lakeland owes its appearance to volcanoes, glaciers and the Cumbrian sheep farmer. The volcanoes provided the tough Borrowdale volcanic rock of which most of the central fells are made, and the glaciers carved the valleys, radiating from a central dome like the spokes of a wheel. The sheep farmer has tamed what was left.

One of the first tasks was to enclose and fence the wilderness, and some of this was done when the monasteries were the great local landowners. The walls are built from the native rock, gathered from nearby fields and fells. Here lies the skill, for most of the walls, clinging to the hillsides like long grey caterpillars, are dry-stone walls. No mortar is used, only the rock to form two wall faces with a rubble core between. Here and there a gigantic 'through' stone is placed, going from one side to the other, with a line of stone cams along the top. Built largely during the enclosure period of the early 19th century, the walls climb to fell summits 1000 feet (305 m) or more high, mute testimony to the skills of men who laboured long ago.

With land as rough, soil as thin and climate as wet as those of central Lakeland, sheep and hill cattle have to provide the main source of farming income. The sheep which thrives so well here is the grey-faced Herdwick, unique to the central sheep farms. Its origin is lost in the mists of the past, but its introduction to Lakeland has been attributed to Norse farmers who settled here or to its having been washed ashore from shipwrecks of the Spanish Armada. Tough, surefooted and hardy, the Herdwick will graze on the highest summits, each flock keeping close to its own 'heaf', or regular grazing area. Flock-marking is essential to sort out the strays, and each farm has its own personal earmark and smitmark recorded in the *Shepherd's Guide*.

Shearing takes place about July, often a task shared between neighbours, and clipping time is one of the busiest seasons on the farm. A fleece may weigh around 5 pounds (2 kg) and this strong, coarse, grey wool often ends up as carpet or hard-wearing tweed. Flocks of 500 Herdwick ewes are not uncommon, together with Swaledale and Rough Fell varieties on the farms away from the central mountains. Open days are organised in summer on various farms throughout Lakeland, when visitors are shown over the land and farming methods are explained.

August brings a quieter time in the farming year, when traditional sheepdog trials are held. There are three principal meetings, at Hill Farm near Windermere, Rydal and Patterdale. The competition is to gather, drive and pen about five reluctant and uncooperative sheep. Success demands the utmost in skill and *rapport* between dog and shepherd.

ABOVE LEFT: *Millbeck, at the foot of Harrison Stickle, a typical valley-head farm in Great Langdale.* FAR LEFT: *Middlefell Place, with Bowfell in the distance.* LEFT: *Dry-stone 'gap' walling in Longsleddale. A huge foundation stone is being lifted into place to strengthen the new wall.* RIGHT: *Shearing a Rough Fell ewe at High Underbrow, near Burneside. Approximately 5 pounds (2 kg) of wool are removed at one shearing.*

Ullswater, Thirlmere and Haweswater

Second to Windermere in size, Ullswater is one of the leading lakes for the boating and yachting enthusiast. It extends in three reaches from Pooley Bridge in the north to Glenridding and Patterdale in the south, a distance of over 7 miles (11 km). The Patterdale end of the lake has fine mountain scenery, being encircled by Helvellyn, Fairfield and Place Fell, whilst the richer pastoral landscape of the Eamont Valley is found to the north.

The waterfall of Aira Force is popular with visitors, and from nearby Gowbarrow Park extensive views may be enjoyed in all directions. The lake yacht *Raven* plies in summer between Glenridding, Howtown and Pooley Bridge, and is often used as the starting or finishing point of a day's walking excursion. Few low-level walks in all Lakeland can equal that from Howtown via Sandwick to Patterdale, and the boat trip gives added interest to the outing. The well-wooded shores and steep mountain sides provide ever-changing views, to be seen to perfection in June greenery, or amidst the rich panoply of October colour.

Trout abound in the cool clear waters, and a skilful angler in May or June can often fill his creel. For the naturalist, deer are found in the Martindale Common area, whilst buzzards may circle overhead from their fastnesses above the Grisedale or Deepdale valleys. The quiet lake held great attractions for Wordsworth,

and his famous poem 'The Daffodils' is generally recognised as having been written about the wild daffodils along Ullswater's shore.

Thirlmere and Haweswater, whilst 10 miles (16 km) apart and separated by two ranges of hills, are two of the lakes which became the first great reservoirs for Manchester. The former lies alongside the busy Ambleside to Keswick road, but a discerning visitor will choose the peace of a scenic route along the western shore.

On a quiet November afternoon, as darkness falls on Haweswater, one may be forgiven for imagining the tolling of a distant bell. Beneath the grey surface of the water lies the drowned valley of Mardale, church, inn and farms all submerged when the original lake was dammed, to provide water for Lancashire's industries almost 90 miles (145 km) away. Remote on the eastern fringe of Lakeland, the Haweswater valley still holds some of its former peace, guarded by the crags around High Street, unchanged since traversed by Roman soldiers almost 2000 years ago.

ABOVE: *Typical autumn colours around the shore of Ullswater.* TOP CENTRE: *Wordsworth's daffodils by Ullswater.* TOP RIGHT: *Autumn mists clear over Thirlmere, looking towards Armboth Fell on the west side of the lake.* RIGHT: *The sparkling waters of a mountain stream flow into the southern end of Haweswater, at the start of their journey to supply water to Manchester.*

Summer Shows and Fairs

Village shows and fairs are an attractive summer feature in the Lakeland valleys. Often based on the local farming background, they can usually be visited in late summer and early autumn.

Sheep classes, especially for the native Herdwick, are many and varied. The 'Blue Riband' for a hill farmer is to win at places like Eskdale, Wasdale and Lowick. Cattle come into their own at Broughton, Cartmel and little Loweswater. Black and white Friesians take pride of place, flanked by huge beef animals like Herefords and Charolais. Horse and pony classes are common, often combined with local show jumping events.

Times past are sometimes recalled with displays of vintage farm equipment and machinery, lovingly restored by proud owners. A team of ornamental plough horses may be seen on occasion, bedecked in brasses and rosettes. Sheep dog trials often link with the shows, attracting shepherds and their dogs from miles around to compete in the open classes.

ABOVE LEFT: *Herdwick sheep await judging at Eskdale Show in West Cumbria.* ABOVE RIGHT: *September sunshine at Loweswater near Cockermouth.* LEFT: *A team of plough horses taking part in a 'vintage' show at Beetham.*

Places to Visit

Many stately homes with attractive gardens exist in and around Lakeland, ranging from small farmhouses of the Middle Ages to huge castles built and restored over many centuries.

The following list of some man-made attractions includes places outside the Lake District but within easy reach of it. Up-to-date information about times of opening, etc., can be had from local tourist offices.

CENTRAL LAKELAND

Houses

Belle Isle on Windermere. Circular 18th-century house with Adam interior and Romney portraits.

Brantwood, by Coniston Water. Home of John Ruskin.

Dove Cottage, Grasmere. Home of William Wordsworth.

Hill Top Farm, Near Sawrey. Home of Beatrix Potter.

Rydal Mount, near Ambleside. Wordsworth's last home.

Townend, Troutbeck. 17th-century farmhouse with original furnishings.

Gardens

Holehird, near Windermere.

Stagshaw, near Ambleside.

Hayes Nurseries, Ambleside.

Museums and Visitor Centres

Brockhole, National Park Visitor Centre, near Windermere.

Grizedale Forest Visitor Centre, near Hawkshead.

Windermere Steamboat Museum, Windermere.

Wordsworth Museum, Town End, Grasmere.

Nature Trails

Belle Isle Nature Trail, on Windermere.

Brantwood Nature Trail, by Coniston Water.

Brockhole Nature Trail, near Windermere.

Claife Heights Nature Trail, near Sawrey.

Millwood Forest Trail, Grizedale.

The Silurian Way, Grizedale.

NORTH LAKELAND

Castle and Cathedral

Carlisle Castle. 12th-century keep, 13th-century gatehouse.

Carlisle Cathedral. Norman and Early English, with magnificent 14th-century east end.

Gardens

Corby Castle, Wetheral, near Carlisle.

Lingholm, by Derwentwater.

Museums and Visitor Centre

Border Regiment Museum, Carlisle.

Carlisle Museum. Cumbrian natural history, archaeology (especially the Roman wall), and fine arts.

Fitz Park Museum, Keswick. Manuscripts of Southey, Wordsworth, Coleridge and Walpole, and local geology and natural history.

Thornthwaite Visitor Centre, Whinlatter Pass, near Keswick. Forest trails and displays of forestry landscapes and life.

Nature and Town Trails

Town Centre Trail, Carlisle.

Dodd Wood Forest Trail, near Keswick.

TOP: *The west wing of Holker Hall, near Grange-over-Sands. Every summer the extensive gardens, which have rare shrubs and trees, are the setting for the Lakeland Rose Show. Visitors to the house can see fine paintings, furnishings and wood-carvings.*
ABOVE: *The garden of Levens Hall, south of Kendal, is outstanding, with topiary work on yew trees and paths laid out in the original 17th-century pattern. The magnificent Elizabethan mansion has ornamental panelling, plasterwork and furniture.*

Eden Riverside Trail, Carlisle.
Launchy Ghyll Forest Trail, near Keswick.
Whinlatter Forest Trail, near Keswick.

SOUTH LAKELAND
Castles, Houses and Priory
Cartmel Priory. Church of 12th-century foundation, with fine 15th-century carving; impressive 14th-century gatehouse.
Holker Hall, Cark-in-Cartmel. *See photo, p. 31.*
Kendal Castle. Ruined birthplace of Catherine Parr, dating from 12th century onwards.
Levens Hall, near Kendal. *See photo, p. 31.*
Rusland Hall, near Ulverston. Georgian, features mechanical music in 18th-century surroundings.
Sizergh Castle, near Kendal. 14th-century pele tower, with 15th-century great hall, and later additions.
Swarthmoor Hall, Ulverston. Elizabethan home of George Fox, who founded the Society of Friends.
Gardens
Graythwaite Hall, near Newby Bridge.
Holker Hall, Cark-in-Cartmel.
Levens Hall, near Kendal.
Art Gallery and Museums
Abbot Hall Art Gallery, Kendal. Georgian building featuring 18th-century furniture and paintings, including Romney's *The Gower Family.*
Kendal Museum. Outstanding mammal and bird collection, local geology and relics of early man.
Museum of Lakeland Life and Industry, Kendal.
Nature and Town Trails
Arnside Knott Nature Trail, Arnside.
Town Centre Trail, Barrow-in-Furness.
Furness Abbey Town Trail, near Barrow-in-Furness.
Hampsfell Nature Trail, Grange-over-Sands.
Hay Bridge Nature Trail, Bouth, near Ulverston.
A Walk Round Kendal.

EAST LAKELAND
Castles and Houses
Appleby Castle. Norman keep and medieval buildings; conservation centre for rare British farm animals.

Brough Castle, near Kirkby Stephen. Norman keep on a Roman site, with later additions.
Brougham Castle, near Penrith. Ruined 12th-century keep and other buildings on the site of a Roman fort.
Dalemain, near Penrith. Medieval, Elizabethan and Georgian house; agricultural and yeomanry museums.
Hutton-in-the-Forest, near Penrith. 14th-century pele tower, with later additions; pictures, tapestries, furniture and gardens.
Garden
Acorn Bank, Temple Sowerby, near Penrith.
Nature and Town Trails
Appleby Castle Nature Trail; Appleby Town Trail.

WEST LAKELAND
Castles and House
Cockermouth Castle. 13th- and 14th-century ruins.
Egremont Castle. Early Norman site. 12th-century ruins.
Muncaster Castle, near Ravenglass. *See photo above.*
Wordsworth House, Cockermouth. Poet's birthplace.
Museum
Whitehaven Museum. Archaeology, industrial history, geology, mining and nautical items.
Nature and Town Trails
Town Walk, Cockermouth.
Nine Becks Walk, Ennerdale.
Smithy Beck Nature Trail, Ennerdale.
Stanley Ghyll Nature Trail, Eskdale.
Town and Harbour Walk, Maryport.
Tree and Nature Trail, Muncaster Castle.
Town Walk, Whitehaven.

ABOVE: *Muncaster Castle. One of Europe's finest collections of rhododendrons and azaleas is among its attractions, as well as fine tapestries, furniture, paintings and porcelain. From the bird garden and nature trails there are magnificent views across the Esk valley.*

ISBN 0 85372 248 X